The Tautology of Water

The Tautology of Water

by Giovanni Boskovich

~ 2025 ~

The Tautology of Water
© Copyright 2025 Mark Danowsky
All rights reserved. No part of this book may be used or reproduced in any manner whatsoever without written permission from either the author or the publisher, except in the case of credited epigraphs or brief quotations embedded in articles or reviews.

Editor-in-chief
Eric Morago

Operations Associate
Shelly Holder

Associate Editors
Mackensi E. Green
Ellen Webre
Allysa Murray

Editor Emeritus
Michael Miller

Front cover art
Eric Morago

Book design
Michael Wada

Moon Tide logo design
Abraham Gomez

Take Care
is published by Moon Tide Press

Moon Tide Press
6709 Washington Ave. #9297
Whittier, CA 90608
www.moontidepress.com

FIRST EDITION

Printed in the United States of America

ISBN # 978-1-957799-34-6

For Emma

Contents

I.

Ophelia, Imagined Somewhere in Los Angeles	11
Drowning	12
Lines Composed Above Cabrillo Beach	13
L.A. as Revenant	14
Yen	15
Folkways	16
Littoral View	17
Caustics	18
September	19
710 North	20
Emotional Commute	21
Sign of the Cross	22
Airport Esperanto	23
Love Hotel	24

II.

Time Regained	28
Proust, Imagined	29
Lavender Tea	30
Dune-buggy Blues	31
Harry Crews in New York	32
Cassavetes' Underpainting	33

III.

Sonnet	36
Brooklyn Sabbatical	37
Midnight Fugue	38
Cherries	39
California Lawns	40
Colloquy	41
South Pasadena Repast	42
Reading & Rereading	43
The Even Years in the Valley	44

IV.

Sardine di Notte	46
The Santa Maria	47
After-Image	48
Fetishism	49
Hospice	50
Gemelli Veneziani	51
Naples (for Cookie Mueller)	53
Villanelle	54
About the Author	56
Acknowledgements	57

I am sleepy and the oozy weeds about me twist.

— Herman Melville

I.

Ophelia, Imagined Somewhere in Los Angeles

You've had too much to drink — not to mention the black-market powder, the name of which changes like the tide: licit one day, illicit the next. Ophelia, you drowned in a kidney-shaped swimming pool, indifferent maids, undocumented and paid cash (under-the-table), just off the clock, sitting at a conspicuously placed bus stop in a tony neighborhood somewhere in the hills (*you choose; it doesn't matter*). No one uses these public reliquaries, the bus stops, that is — the help, according to the rich, are only synecdochically relevant (*e.g.*, lend me a hand, an ear, perambulate my children, teach them your tongue; hold yours, etc). I've never seen a rich person use the bus in these sinuous hills, especially in Los Angeles, a place where cars (new, semi-electric, electric, imagined, flying, classic, lowrider, jalopy, 80s, Yotas) are all better than schlepping the bus. I eye them as I drive through these hills towards San Pedro. And you, Ophelia: No self-coronated diadem of nettles or daisies. *Too much water.* Bougainvillea, whispering with sibilance, watched you (the maids, as I said, are waiting for their respective terminuses: Carson, San Pedro, Wilmington), heavy with drink, as you mermaided your way to the deep end, like lagan, for us to find you, again and again.

Drowning

Situated in folding-chair leisure
a retired fisherman
lay asleep —
postprandial, perhaps —
head lolling
like slack tide
towards the salubrious
chlorinated water.

A jacuzzi is an ironic place
for a bathetic drowning;
or an equally absurd saving.

A nonswimmer,
I slipped,
submarining
a half-fathom's depth,
before my grandfather
pulled me up, light, like the nets
I watched him work by hand.

Lines Composed Above Cabrillo Beach

A swath of birds
sits upon a becalmed sea,
a respite from the doldrums
of transpacific travel.
These creatures rest,
husbanding energy,
snorkeling for snacks,
mackerel, small fish.

A dolphin party appears
fashionably late
for the binoculared man
who, with morning coffee,
vacillates between newspaper
and sea-news.
Ocean headlines say:
Area Dolphins Frolic
While White Crane
Alights on Abalone Shell.

A lone surfer drifts out,
each wave a comma,
or whispered parentheses.

Perhaps nature will usurp man
and dolphins will reign supreme
and the white-craned question mark
of the bird's neck will ask us:

What now?
What now, creatures?

L.A. as Revenant

A lambent wave laps
at the morning shore
whose ebbing tide draws
bathers like an anchor to its depths.

And another! this one foamy,
crests like a marmoreal Bernini,
as a sunbather manages,
through her beach fatigue,
to sit-up, linking sound and vision.

Doyen surfers slap stomachs to wax
and drop into satori.
Debouching McClure Tunnel,
blinded by Southern California light
that throws no shadow,
these westerners swim
with the desert at their backs.

This is no ersatz landscape.
No unreality here.

It's a prickly pear.
A eucalyptus tree.
A right-hand point break
for the laborers, lawyers, Malibu rentiers —
western-minded folks who,
supine on beach towels,
or prostrate on surfboards,
worship this desert on the shore.

Yen

The architecture of the ocean
bequeaths something to the builder's imagination,
with his yen for size, the shapely,
the astrophic building of stanzas.

A wave, cresting into an Ionian column,
cantilevers over a surfer
who feverishly paddles for the outside
but as fate will have it, he's subsumed
onto the floor of the sea.

This tumult, though, subsides into clarity —
a carte-blanche, limpid sea
that leaves folks on shore, hungry for these once-seen
vertiginous heights, shoulders, clean lines.

Without this ebb, this iron-pressed sea,
can we imagine these heights, declensions?
What is this colloquy between absence and presence?

Folkways

The folkways of surfers are arcane,
near-occult business
performed as if by shroud of night,
yet in the wantonness of daylight.

For some, their gestures
are hermetic shorthand —
like cypher dug into sand,
only to be deciphered before
the erasure of high tide.

Tucked away in the womb
of some peninsular cove
overlooking a corduroy sea,
they denude themselves.

And at sunset, they doff their neoprene,
a cigarette balanced between their lips,
with the same aplomb as walking the nose;
their on-shore gesticulations
a kind of skywriting that limns
a summary of the day.

Littoral View

Littoral views of the 101
on a good day —
somewhere, northbound
between Malibu
and Pleasure Point:
one-night motels
pointillism of sand-speckled feet,
surfboard-stacked Toyotas.

And yet, like a parallax view,
it's the Irish coastline —
leviathan island
knitted in with fog,
a veiled mystery,
a turgid seaman's corpse.

The causeway between
the parking-lot towel-changer
and the nimbus of seabirds
in the Irish mist
is merely an incisive view.

Caustics

Tracing the lines of a cordillera
with her camera,
she piously colors its beauty
like an innocent confessant
tonguing the host.

And although she protests that it pales,
the arid watercolors of her photograph
somehow capture more than the thing itself.

Like learning the word of a thing you've seen
yet never known.

Like caustics —
those reflective lines
in a swimming pool
that, as a child, I stared at in wonder,
their kaleidoscopic meanderings
shifting as the sun sank into its nadir,
demarcating the day's end.

It merely adds to the wonder,
placing a name into an empty placeholder.

You, the sought-after word
in a dictionary, always there.

Embayed in your prelapsarian L.A.,
you traded it for Big Sur —
circuitous roads, cliffsides,
spindrift, burnt-out surfers, margin-riders.

But even in L.A.,
vestigial desert underfoot,
its name forgotten
(*El Pueblo de Nuestra Señora...*),
you could have uncovered
what was there all along.

September

       Two monarch butterflies — *two!* —
      blew right in front of my '63 Falcon,
          auguring psychic calm
           somewhere ahead —
       perhaps on this peninsular
          two-lane highway
  that takes me to my favorite beach
      monikered by the locals
           as Sand Hill.

710 North

A graffito that reads like the opening credits of a film says, character by character — each letter taking a parapet of the freeway overpass — CRASH. It becomes a refrain, like some one-word rhythm, an obsession. The Clear Channel billboard is subsumed in this mantra of death. CRASH. A woman applies her makeup in the sun-visor, glancing the imperative, as she limns crimson onto her lips. Car-insurance billboards predict the future like a ziggurat of unread tarot cards: a concatenation of cars piling up like a vehicular sacrifice to the freeway gods. At least this one-note dirge, CRASH, doesn't obfuscate: it exhorts, cajoles, teases, nudges us towards swinging the steering wheel into the mother or student-driver or teenager in the next lane. The Clear Channel billboard peddles death but is nothing short of meretricious. What else is this cast of lawyers doing, with their dollar-sign rictuses, but indiscriminately incanting our collective deaths.

Emotional Commute

In L.A. I drive with my foot on the brake,
slightly depressed, an almost-there, spectral touch,
and I merge with my eyes on the rearview —
the chiasmus of the 405 and the 110
signaling the dénouement of my drive.

Movie-ending sunset, *sulla destra*,
sfumatos into the Santa Monica Bay.

Every driver, a would-be accident.
Every car a metonym for success, failure;
a mobile topographic pushpin on a map:
Inglewood, Hawthorne, Gardena,
Carson, Wilmington, San Pedro.
 I was once rear-ended on the 710 North,
so close to work (*it always happens close to your destination*, they say).
The driver, illicitly borrowed his grandmother's car
and pleaded with me to say that she was driving, not him,
to my insurance. It's always someone else's fault.

Sign of the Cross

Sometimes, before merging onto the Arroyo,
or boarding a plane, I furtively
make the sign of the Cross,
Cradle Catholic that I am.

Other times, perhaps during an early morning surf,
you're there, occluded like a shark in high tide,
preying on me, while I pray for a wave
to carry me to terra firma,
away from that littoral nightmare.

Sometimes, too, when I'm really in-tune
I can even admit that I miss you —
the way your wet hair looked after a shower;
or the urbane way you read,
feet curled on the chair like a recumbent snake;
and your weird hermitic hippie meals,
the ones I complained about
yet now can't find the recipes
for the life of me.

Even now, parenthetical cross,
my secreted memories of you
ineluctably rise, like lagan, to the surface.

Airport Esperanto

The photos themselves whisper
some kind of airport Esperanto —
Fiumicino, Gatwick, Tegel.

Your eyes pray
the customs officer likes palaver
as latitudinal sweat
runs down your face.

Customs Declaration Tableau
(promptly filled out prior to deboarding):

> • *If I Die in the Combat Zone, Box Me Up and Ship Me Home*
> • Hasselblad 500C
> • Ry Cooder's *Paradise and Lunch*
> • Charles Schulz ephemera

You lie and tick *'No'* for the box that says:
(d) soil or have been on a farm/ranch/pasture.

I once waited three hours in the LAX loop,
tattooing the upholstery, cigarette in mouth,
wondering if you'd make it through customs.

You said the Customs Man small-talked
then let you slide into
a Hollywood sunset —
some near-crash
on the Arroyo
as you, driver's side,
photograph the San Gabriel Mountains
with a billboard caesura extolling
the virtues of cheap car insurance.

Love Hotel

I.

The Proustian waiter is on loan —
not from the Louvre,
but from a non-existent
arrondissement of Paris:
Saint Martin-cum-Sint Maarten.

We came as an untaxed import
from Los Angeles,
a place where chevrons of pelicans
soar like bubbles in
French-imported rosé.

Tacit guilt is reflected in Euro-tendered cocktails,
served by the flotsam of colonization.

No khaki-clad white skin here, though:
these folks are all tanned and stand-up paddle board
to offshore schooners that take tourists
on hundred-Euro cruises in the crepuscular Caribbean.

And although the brochure
advertised a room
with a view of Grand Case's waters,
it was instead flanked by open-edifice buildings,
where inside, visible to the tourist's eye,
St. Martiners played cards
and smoked two-Euro cigarettes,
ironically called *News*.

II.

One night, I sat in a tourist-trap called *Calm Cafe*,
while a cover band played "Stir It Up" and Floridians sipped
cartoon-sized cocktails. Next to me was Kali, a true Carib.

Everyone knows me! I'm Kali! You come to my restaurant,
it's past the post office, it's called Kali's Cafe, I named it after me.
Bienvenue! You want weed, man? I get you weed.
Watch this — hey, you!

Kali moved his weed-grinder like a sundial,
crushing his island weed into a sand
that was falling all around his feet.
Kali was drunk, but then again, so was I.
Finally, he said, *You come to Kali's, I'll treat you like a king.*

But there were enough kings in Saint Martin at one time,
so I never visited Kali, instead staying at the Love Hotel,
where Frenchmen poured white sangria,
on moon-shaped tables
so tourists, like me, could sip cocktails
in shallow water.

II.

Time Regained

It took the beginning
and end of two relationships
to finish Proust
(Eve Babitz, it is said, read all of it
in a Los Angeles laundromat).
By *Time Regained*
I'd lost one to indifference,
another I sacrificed.
The irony, however,
is not not lost on me,
that I could —
if time were truly regained —
use the wisdom gleaned
to rectify my errors,
my little jealousies.

Proust, Imagined

Proust would have eschewed internet use,
a digital footprint ebbed away at low tide.

Salubrious Balbec is better than the
marmoreal waters of the Rockaways.

The psychic realms of healing:
thermal springs of Ischia, never visited;
Jeffers' Big Sur; peninsular Palos Verdes.
At night, I intone a spiritual addendum to a familiar prayer,
All water is tautological.

Lavender Tea

She listens to *Metal Machine Music*
sipping lavender tea,
reading the Sunday paper.

This, she says,
is her way of having space,
the solitude of morning.

She smokes a cigarette —
perhaps two —
then finishes her tea.

Dune-buggy Blues

>Manson adumbrated
>that the world would end,
>but instead
>it just goes on
>and on
>and on.

Harry Crews in New York

I've been trying to escape the New York of the Mind.
Geographically I'm here in Los Angeles
and I got rid of you, vestigial New York.
Not that I miss you,
it's just that the other day
I thought of my first New York snow
falling in Park Slope.
I was entrenched in a cafe
reading Harry Crews,
another *Escape from New York*.
Even a southerner like Crews
was a respite from the chisel of New York:
he's all dog fights, hot dogs, dildos, and snakes.

And now I'm trying to escape
the New York of the Mind.
Coney Island of the Mind.
We went there just before
the plague took the masses
and then took us, too.

I was trying to get back to L.A.
and rid myself of you,
Coney Island Baby,
the last bit of New York
that still clings to my clothes
my onanistic dreams
and my books
and my records
and my solitary drives
and my swims in the Pacific Ocean,
not so pacific anymore.

Cassavetes' Underpainting

Cassavetes' unseen
footage is an underpainting,
a spectral presence,
like the first time I noticed
that half-limned woman
in Courbet's *Burial at Ornan*
at Musée d'Orsay,
up until that point, undetectable,
in gift-shop postcards,
and reproductions.

Cassavetes could skeletonize
or apotheosize
the everyday in Los Angeles,
right there in his at-home
movie studio,
a Moviola parked
in lieu of a car.

III.

Sonnet

The tonsuring of middle age
comes suddenly
and against our will,
like a father

forcing a son
into the barber's chair.
The freshly cut hair,
tear-soaked paper-mâché.

The barber, flanked by his tools —
disinfectant, shears, clippers —
hands the boy a mirror,
framing him in a mise-en-abyme.

How do you like it, the father asks?
as the boy looks down, noting what's lost.

Brooklyn Sabbatical

A dog barks
while somewhere
the sun sets upon a corrugated sea,
lambent like ebbed-up abalone.

These trees
are the same as those
old-man limbs
across town
that reach up
for that last bit of sun.

Yet, here, the flotsam of cigarettes
reads differently:
a little less legibly;
the trash a Tower of Babel;
the treble of sirens
traveling as routinely
as a subway timetable
from terminus
to necropolis.

In a Park Avenue apartment:
a small child sits down for piano lessons.

The compass of that disc
rises, nevertheless, on both sides —
living, moribund, dead —
with all of us wondering,
in this daily dance of katabasis,
what it's like above
and below.

Midnight Fugue

In the train station of dreams
there you were:
seated alone, eying the platform.

Your journey, ahead of you,
somehow complete:
two superimposed temporal realms.

> You and your partner —
> his nebulous face,
> a star chart of ex-boyfriends
> alchemized into one —
> sat across from another couple
> traveling in tandem,
> a sign of advanced intimacy.

I was both present and future,
cool, unbiased.

> Asking the obvious
> you said: *No*
> but then yes: *We are together.*

I alighted your train,
half-watching it disappear.

> Life holds, within its two hands,
> limitless possibilities,
> yet they can all be sorted into two:
> arrivals and departures.

Cherries

Like pits and uneaten cherries
in the same bowl
the detritus of our bad habits
dialogue with our good ones.

California Lawns

Moving the sprinkler every five minutes
she thinks to herself,
How could I have let it get this bad.

Carrying the sprinkler to another half-dirt section,
she listlessly open-palms it onto the ground.

Two-fingered, she powders
the dregs of her coffee onto the grass,
terminus of her morning.

Could this be morning?
What is matutinal about endings?
Who, too, is absent from this painting,
as morning sfumatos into afternoon,
youth into middle-age?

Colloquy

the algebra of birds' wings,
simple yet complex
quotidian like framed needle-point art
hanging there, on the wall,
since time immemorial

i tell my friend,
a physics instructor, Cosmin,
that formulas and brain gestures
pervert nature's inherent beauty

it all pulls back the curtain,
the rip in the stocking,
big toe peeking out of the sock

to which he replies:
i disagree;
it *is* nature, Giovanni.

South Pasadena Repast

South Pasadena, I used to live here,
amongst your alarm-clock parrots,
Caribbean green and red.
Today, like a child coming home,
I returned to your bosom
of craftsman homes
and single-bar Mission Street.
I heard Chopin's "Polonaise in A-flat Major"
as I walked up to the coffee shop,
soon-to-be re-read comic in hand,
to find a homeless man,
all Satie monochromatic black.
I asked, *Is that Chopin?*
Yes, he replied.
I pointed to his bounty,
a five-dollar bill, creased down the middle,
on the floor next to the outdoor piano
noting, *You lost a fiver.*
He picked it up and said,
I hope I didn't lose all my money.

Reading & Rereading

Perhaps if I read one more novel
a tome, a corpus — Cervantes, Proust, all of the Brontë Sisters? —
I might have enough ink to write my own work;
or at least cast off the lassitude of this
intellectual winter.

When did Joyce know that he came into his own,
his epiphanic moment?
Or did crepuscule creep
into Zürich, unannounced,
with the dimmer.
Perhaps Nora told him.

One knows, though, that they must never
compare themselves to the leviathans of literature.
Yet we all do it — across disciplines,
time zones. Compare ourselves to the dead.

I promised myself
I wouldn't buy any more books
until I read each and every one
on my shelf.

Or maybe I'll get around to writing
when I've *reread*
all of the books
in my house.

Or perhaps once I finish
grading these papers.

But I forget,
so I tell myself:
this is my house;
I'm already here.

The Even Years in the Valley

Having internally mantracized
Even years are the best years
he approached thirty six,
its metrical cretic valley,
like a hermitage:
the puerilism of his twenties
behind him,
attic forties ahead.

It's here, however, in this valley, that he waits,
soul slackening
like the postprandial unnotching of a belt.

Thirty, when turned on its side,
resembles a numerical valley.
A geographical depression.
The cordillera of time,
notwithstanding our misgivings,
beckons us to climb its sides.

IV.

Sardine di Notte

Freshly caught sardines
on the BBQ
at midnight.

A small seaside village
in Palermo, 1940.

Un fidanzato whistles
for his beloved,
secondo piano.

A watchful mother approves:
Scendi le scale.

The Santa Maria

My grandfather, it is said, was already working
on a fishing boat by the age of eight.
The flotsam and vestigial oral history is now
what I sift through as I limn my crude painting of him,
there in Sicily. Second-, third-hand narratives
my grandmother or uncles shared —
tales of bravery, poise, and charity. These tales spill,
porous, into my dreams and woolgathering.

And now, like some Chandlerian shamus tracing over paper
in search of long-lost handwriting, I find traces of myself.

No spurious yarn (I have the newspaper, sepia with age).
An Italian-run fishing boat, the Santa Maria via San Pedro,
caught fire off the coast of Baja. Yet before the conflagration
consumed the boat, its catch and crew, my grandfather, privy
that the Mexican deckhands couldn't swim,
tied them to the nets' floats, saving all of their lives.

The Santa Maria, consumed in flames, its crew, floated
appositionally.

Although gone a nearly two decades,
he is somewhere, traced under me like a palimpsest;
and indeed he comes out, revenant,
but this time not as a theophanic miracle
of saving drowning fishermen
but in more reticent ways,
like an unseen bird, floating
in the California gloam.

After-Image

My grandfather
centrifugally peeling
pears at evening's repast,
just the two of us,
my grandmother
watching telenovelas
in the other room.

Between us,
ersatz wooden fruit,
silent, dark-umbered,
like a Chardin still-life.

As the crayon-red
knife handle
deftly maelstroms
the rind,
the left thumb
backpedaling
close behind,
he halves the fruit,
passing it to me,
thus ending
our night ritual.

Fetishism

Holding her needle in the lingerie factory
like a stranger's rosary, my grandmother —
an inveterate Catholic and Sicilian immigrant —
pierces the fabric that resembles antimacassar,
all-white holes holding their own
intentionality of intimacy.

And they are, indeed, to be donned
but by women, thronged by nighttime
in some midwestern motel —
or, perhaps, a birthday or tender-kissed anniversary.
 I wonder if my grandmother Nunzia
noted the irony in her work:
Did she know, for example,
that these garments,
would be donned and denuded
for annual demimondes?

And did the wearers,
lost in fetishism,
know that at the other end,
women had performed
an entirely different
labor power?

Hospice

Rosary beads, talcum powder,
cough drops; an invalid's gold bell.

My grandmother tells me,
through the waterfall of slanted light,
that the saints have forgotten her.

Gemelli Veneziani

Years ago, on a redeye from Honolulu to L.A.
I was seated next to Venetian twins,
retiree antique dealers with a large *magazzino*
filled with miscellany: antiquated books,
armor redolent of Wolfram von Eschenbach,
top-40 Italian records — viz, cultural flotsam.

Wielding my Sicilian, they giggled
at *Idda*, correcting it
like a linguistics professor
into *Lei* for me. The more talkative one,
Flavia, asked what Italian authors I liked,
and I verbally indexed a few:
Ginzberg, Pirandello, Tabucchi.

After the pre-flight palaver and cabin lights dimmed,
I fell asleep, only to be awakened
by the pilot announcing that one of the engines
had failed (my mother's twin had died
as a mere infant years before in Sicily,
a casualty of meningitis and inchoate health care).
I then carefully explained the situation to the twins,
who maintained their customary northern equanimity.

Shuttled back to the Waikiki,
I helped situate them
into the airline's one-night
mia culpa stay at the Ala Moana.

The next morning, we met under
a ceiling-hung outrigger and had breakfast
while sorting out their canceled flights
since they couldn't speak a lick of English.

Back home in South Pasadena,
I received a surprise package filled with
hardbound Italian-language novels
by the writers I'd rattled off on the plane.

Seven years later,
and a two-year caesura
of a Boccaccian plague,
I saw those twins; this time,
however, on the island of Venice.
They drove me to Mestre,
a few kilometers outside
the floating city,
because as most locals know,
there isn't a decent meal
to be found in Venice.

Naples (for Cookie Mueller)

The energy here is like a bar at 2am,
I tell her — pending violence.
We witnessed two fights
in thirty minutes;
and yet, I feel at home
here in Naples.

Pyramidal trash piles,
concatenation clothes lines,
deep-fried anchovies,
and a for-sale octopus
marooned in a kiddie pool.

Just a vaporetto away
from my homeland of Sicily,
Naples elicits
a frisson of terror
and pleasure.
The Strait of Messina,
the lacuna
separating
these people
from my own.

And this, perhaps, is why
we have chosen this
as our terminus of tourism.

Villanelle

I went swimming in the mercury
the horizon and welkin
touching, no longer discrete.

A checkmark of pelicans
clarifying the liminal,
I went swimming in the mercury.

The sargassum, tangled,
byzantine, all around me,
touching, no longer discrete.

Above, frustrating satori,
a police helicopter (LAPD), hovering;
I went swimming in the mercury.

And the water, all around me,
cool, approaches equinoctial,
touching, no longer discrete.

Even here, in becalmed waters,
human din creeps in,
while swimming in the mercury,
touching, no longer discrete.

About the Author

Giovanni Boskovich (b. 1985) is a poet and educator born and raised in San Pedro, California. He holds an MA in Literature from California State University Dominguez Hills where he published a thesis on Emily Dickinson. His work has appeared in *California Quarterly, Arteidolia Press*, the *Santa Barbara Literary Journal, Big Windows Review, POETiCA REVIEW,* and *Broken Lens Journal.* In his free time, he surfs anywhere from Cabrillo Beach to Baja, Mexico.

Acknowledgements

Grateful acknowledgement is made to the following publications, in which some of these poems first appeared: "Lines Composed Above Cabrillo Beach," *California Quarterly;* "Ophelia, Imagined Somewhere in Los Angeles," "Sonnet," "Drowning," *Santa Barbara Literary Journal;* "Cassavetes' Underpainting," "Cherries," "Lavender Tea," *Arteidolia Press;* "Naples, For Cookie Mueller," *Broken Lens Journal.*

This book, which began as a way of reconnecting with my native Los Angeles after a yearlong maelstrom in New York, would not be possible without the support of many wonderful people. I must first thank Dr. Jon Hauss, the literary wellspring, for his friendship and limitless knowledge that he has bestowed upon me over the years.

I must also thank my dear friend of fifteen years over in Portsmouth, England, James Sharp, for his creative bravery and daily emotional support when life — and the book — seemed daunting or impossible.

For sundry and equally important reasons, the following people deserve my deepest gratitude: Susana Gonzalez, Nathaniel Fregoso, Sara Litman, Clark Allen, Marshall Dahlin, Michael Trejo, Rainer Werner Fassbinder, Gena Rowlands, Denny Bales, Jon Mangiagli, Hudson Ritchie, and Eric Morago at Moon Tide Press for believing in this paean to Los Angeles.

I also owe a massive amount of thanks to my family, living and deceased, for being there for me along the way. Finally, I must thank my wife, Emma, for supporting me during this process, and most importantly, all things in life.

Also Available from Moon Tide Press

Take Care, Mark Danowsky (2025)
Dilapitatia, Kelly Gray (2025)
Reluctant Prophets, J.D. Isip (2025)
Enormous Blue Umbrella, Donna Hilbert (2025)
Sky Leaning Toward Winter, Terri Niccum (2024)
Living the Sundown: A Caregiving Memoir, G. Murray Thomas (2024)
Figure Study, Kathryn de Lancellotti (2024)
Suffer for This: Love, Sex, Marriage, & Rock 'N' Roll,
    Victor D. Infante (2024)
What Blooms in the Dark, Emily J. Mundy (2024)
Fable, Bryn Wickerd (2024)
Diamond Bars 2, David A. Romero (2024)
Safe Handling, Rebecca Evans (2024)
More Jerkumstances: New & Selected Poems,
    Barbara Eknoian (2024)
Dissection Day, Ally McGregor (2023)
He's a Color Until He's Not, Christian Hanz Lozada (2023)
The Language of Fractions, Nicelle Davis (2023)
Paradise Anonymous, Oriana Ivy (2023)
Now You Are a Missing Person, Susan Hayden (2023)
Maze Mouth, Brian Sonia-Wallace (2023)
Tangled by Blood, Rebecca Evans (2023)
Another Way of Loving Death, Jeremy Ra (2023)
Kissing the Wound, J.D. Isip (2023)
Feed It to the River, Terhi K. Cherry (2022)
Beat Not Beat: An Anthology of California Poets S
    crewing on the Beat and Post-Beat Tradition (2022)
When There Are Nine: Poems Celebrating the
    Life and Achievements of Ruth Bader Ginsburg (2022)
The Knife Thrower's Daughter, Terri Niccum (2022)
2 Revere Place, Aruni Wijesinghe (2022)
Here Go the Knives, Kelsey Bryan-Zwick (2022)
Trumpets in the Sky, Jerry Garcia (2022)
Threnody, Donna Hilbert (2022)
A Burning Lake of Paper Suns, Ellen Webre (2021)
Instructions for an Animal Body, Kelly Gray (2021)

Head *V* Heart: New & Selected Poems, Rob Sturma (2021)
Sh!t Men Say to Me: A Poetry Anthology in Response to Toxic Masculinity (2021)
Flower Grand First, Gustavo Hernandez (2021)
Everything is Radiant Between the Hates, Rich Ferguson (2020)
When the Pain Starts: Poetry as Sequential Art, Alan Passman (2020)
This Place Could Be Haunted If I Didn't Believe in Love, Lincoln McElwee (2020)
Impossible Thirst, Kathryn de Lancellotti (2020)
Lullabies for End Times, Jennifer Bradpiece (2020)
Crabgrass World, Robin Axworthy (2020)
Contortionist Tongue, Dania Ayah Alkhouli (2020)
The only thing that makes sense is to grow, Scott Ferry (2020)
Dead Letter Box, Terri Niccum (2019)
Tea and Subtitles: Selected Poems 1999-2019, Michael Miller (2019)
At the Table of the Unknown, Alexandra Umlas (2019)
The Book of Rabbits, Vince Trimboli (2019)
Everything I Write Is a Love Song to the World, David McIntire (2019)
Letters to the Leader, HanaLena Fennel (2019)
Darwin's Garden, Lee Rossi (2019)
Dark Ink: A Poetry Anthology Inspired by Horror (2018)
Drop and Dazzle, Peggy Dobreer (2018)
Junkie Wife, Alexis Rhone Fancher (2018)
The Moon, My Lover, My Mother, & the Dog, Daniel McGinn (2018)
Lullaby of Teeth: An Anthology of Southern California Poetry (2017)
Angels in Seven, Michael Miller (2016)
A Likely Story, Robbi Nester (2014)
Embers on the Stairs, Ruth Bavetta (2014)
The Green of Sunset, John Brantingham (2013)
The Savagery of Bone, Timothy Matthew Perez (2013)
The Silence of Doorways, Sharon Venezio (2013)
Cosmos: An Anthology of Southern California Poetry (2012)
Straws and Shadows, Irena Praitis (2012)
In the Lake of Your Bones, Peggy Dobreer (2012)
I Was Building Up to Something, Susan Davis (2011)
Hopeless Cases, Michael Kramer (2011)

One World, Gail Newman (2011)
What We Ache For, Eric Morago (2010)
Now and Then, Lee Mallory (2009)
Pop Art: An Anthology of Southern California Poetry (2009)
In the Heaven of Never Before, Carine Topal (2008)
A Wild Region, Kate Buckley (2008)
Carving in Bone: An Anthology of Orange County Poetry (2007)
Kindness from a Dark God, Ben Trigg (2007)
A Thin Strand of Lights, Ricki Mandeville (2006)
Sleepyhead Assassins, Mindy Nettifee (2006)
Tide Pools: An Anthology of Orange County Poetry (2006)
Lost American Nights: Lyrics & Poems, Michael Ubaldini (2006)

Patrons

Moon Tide Press would like to thank the following people for their support in helping publish the finest poetry from the Southern California region. To sign up as a patron, visit www.moontidepress.com or send an email to publisher@moontidepress.com.

Anonymous
Robin Axworthy
Conner Brenner
Nicole Connolly
Bill Cushing
Susan Davis
Kristen Baum DeBeasi
Peggy Dobreer
Kate Gale
Dennis Gowans
Alexis Rhone Fancher
HanaLena Fennel
Half Off Books & Brad T. Cox
Donna Hilbert
Jim & Vicky Hoggatt
Michael Kramer
Ron Koertge & Bianca Richards
Gary Jacobelly
Ray & Christi Lacoste
Jeffery Lewis

Zachary & Tammy Locklin
Lincoln McElwee
David McIntire
José Enrique Medina
Michael Miller &
Rachanee Srisavasdi
Michelle & Robert Miller
Ronny & Richard Morago
Terri Niccum
Andrew November
Jeremy Ra
Luke & Mia Salazar
Jennifer Smith
Roger Sponder
Andrew Turner
Rex Wilder
Mariano Zaro
Wes Bryan Zwick